TREVOR ROWLEY and JOHN WOOD

DESERTED VILLAGES

Third edition

D1387027

SHIRE ARCHAEOLOGY

2

941. 009
734 Row

Cover photographs
(Top) Tiantulloch Broch, Scotland. The remains of the circular Iron Age stronghold were
incorporated into a later settlement, itself now deserted.
(Bottom) Easter Raitts, Kingussie, Scotland. A small settlement cleared in the early nineteenth
century to make way for sheep, which has been the subject of excavations by the Highland
Council and the University of Aberdeen.
(Photographs by James Bone, reproduced by courtesy of the Highland Council
and the RCAHMS)

British Library Cataloguing in Publication Data:
Rowley, Trevor. Deserted Villages. - 3rd. ed. - (Shire Archaeology ; 23)
1. Extinct cities – Great Britain
2. Excavations (Archaeology) – Great Britain
3. Great Britain – Antiquities
I. Title II. Wood, John.
941'. 009734.
ISBN 0 7478 0474 5

Published in 2000 by
SHIRE PUBLICATIONS LTD
Cromwell House, Church Street, Princes Risborough,
Buckinghamshire HP27 9AA, UK.
(Website: www.shirebooks.co.uk)

Series Editor: James Dyer.

Number 23 in the Shire Archaeology series.

ISBN 0 7478 0474 5

First published 1982, reprinted 1985. Second edition 1995. Third edition 2000.

Acknowledgements

We have drawn generously on the published works of the great pioneers of the investigation of
deserted villages, Professor M. W. Beresford, Mr J. G. Hurst and Professor W. G. Hoskins, and we
gratefully acknowledge our debt to them. We would particularly like to thank Shirley Hermon for
preparing the typescript and Hilary Welch for drawing the final plans.
We are most grateful to the following for permission to reproduce or redraw their plans: fig. 1,
map revision, from the Medieval Settlement Research Group lists by Robin Glassock with assistance
from Alan Nash, cartography by Michael Young and Pamela Lucas, Department of Geography,
Cambridge University; fig. 3, James Bond; fig. 4, John Steane and James Bond; fig. 17, Phil Page;
and the Cambridge Committee for Aerial Photography for permission to reproduce plates 1, 2, 3,
5, 6, 9, 10, 12, 13, 15, 16, 19; plate 17, Mr R. B. B. Gibbs for photographing the Boarstall map in
the Buckinghamshire Record Office; plate 18, All Souls College, Oxford.
Thanks are also due to Linda Mitchell for preparing the index and Mélanie Steiner for redrawing
some of the plans and correcting the proofs of the revised edition.

Printed in Great Britain by CIT Printing Services Ltd, Press Buildings, Merlins Bridge,
Haverfordwest, Pembrokeshire SA61 1XF.

Contents

Preface

Although the study of deserted villages is relatively young, well over three thousand have been identified in England alone over the past forty years. Many of these have been found by amateurs working as individuals or in groups. It is the aim of this publication to draw attention to this fascinating aspect of the English landscape and to encourage others to visit known sites and discover new ones.

It is our hope too that some readers will be tempted into recording village sites: only a small proportion of known sites have been surveyed even in the most cursory way. The task of making a recording may sound rather daunting, but after a few days experience it becomes a fairly simple and extremely rewarding exercise. However you approach the topic, we hope that deserted villages bring as much pleasure to you as they have to us.

Trevor Rowley, John Wood. *Oxford, 1982.*

Preface to the third edition

In the eighteen years since this book first appeared the study of landscape history has developed considerably, helped by a variety of disciplines. Deserted villages are only one element in a complex story of social and environmental development, but the impressive sites recorded in the English Midlands and Yorkshire by fieldworkers in the 1950s and 1960s have stimulated rural settlement studies throughout the British Isles. Deserted villages of all types and periods still have power to provoke the imagination and provoke further research, and there is still a need to record and study them. Fortunately it is an area of research very much open to the part-time archaeologist and historian equipped with relatively simple, inexpensive equipment.

Trevor Rowley, John Wood. *2000.*

List of illustrations

1
What is a deserted village?

Do deserted villages exist?

'He had heard divers ancient people say and affirm that in old time there was a town within the parish of Middleton called Kiplingcotes. That he hath often seen the plain marks and indication of divers frontsteads and the foundations of divers houses, and also a large hole where there was a well for the use of the inhabitants of Kiplingcotes. There was a chapel, and the lesser of the two bells in Middleton Church was brought thither when the town was demolished.'

Such was the evidence of William Wilkinson, yeoman, in a dispute over tithes in 1689 (Beresford, 1954). The plaintiff was concerned to prove that there had never been a village or church at Kiplingcotes and that no tithes had ever been paid. Another witness to the Kiplingcotes enquiry refused 'to believe that there was ever any such town'. Nevertheless such a village did once exist and had been deserted along with many other settlements during the later middle ages.

Deserted settlements of one kind or another have now been found in virtually every part of the British Isles. Yet only fifty years ago many people were sceptical about their very existence. For example, as recently as 1946 the great economic historian Sir Alfred Clapham remarked: 'Deserted villages are singularly rare in England.' Nevertheless, some had already been identified by local historians in the eighteenth and nineteenth centuries. As early as 1846 the Reverend J. Wilson undertook excavations at the deserted village of Woodperry not far from Oxford.

In Oliver Goldsmith's *The Deserted Village* (1770), the preface was addressed to the sceptics, whose number included Dr Johnson: 'I have taken all possible pains in my country excursions for these four or five years past to be certain of what I allege. Some of my friends think that the depopulation of villages does not exist, but I am myself satisfied.'

It seems that the poem was based on actual experience rather than romantic fantasy. Goldsmith visited Nuneham Courtenay in Oxfordshire at the time that the first Lord Harcourt was levelling the old village and replacing it with a new model village on the line of the present Oxford to Henley road, where regular brick estate cottages can still be seen today. Nuneham was one of very many villages to be moved in the late eighteenth century in order to create or expand landscaped parks.

Deserted villages have been systematically investigated only since the 1950s. Tribute must be paid to the pioneers of deserted village research: Professor M. W. Beresford, whose *Lost Villages of England* appeared in 1954; and Professor W. G. Hoskins, who published *The Making of the English Landscape* the following year. Such scholars laid the solid foundations for subsequent investigation into abandoned rural settlement. The Deserted Medieval Village Research Group, founded in 1952, under the watchful stewardship of its Secretary for over twenty years, Mr J. G. Hurst, helped to stimulate and co-ordinate further investigation. By 1977 the Group had recorded over three thousand deserted villages in England alone (fig. 1). However, it soon became apparent that former settlements could be found almost everywhere. The map was therefore not subsequently updated. The Group's change of name to the Medieval Settlement Research Group reflected a developing awareness by geographers, historians and archaeologists that deserted villages must now be viewed in the context of the continuously evolving landscape.

Deserted villages in the landscape

The term *village* is not an easy one to define. Because of the enormous variety of settlement in the countryside we need to employ a broad definition of *village*, which will enable us to consider hamlets and clusters of farms on the one hand and small towns on the other. In parts of East Anglia and south-west England rural settlement has traditionally been scattered, while in the Midlands agricultural communities have tended to be more compact. For our purpose the *village* will consist of a group of families living in a collection of houses and having a sense of community, irrespective of its actual size.

Settlement history is much more fluid than we might imagine by examining the countryside today. The tranquillity of many villages suggests to the casual observer that they have existed more or less in their present form since they were first established; but the apparent timelessness of many villages is deceptive: prosperous towns can decline, and tiny hamlets grow – settlements are organic and are constantly changing. Villages have prospered, declined and migrated to new sites for a wide variety of social, cultural and economic reasons as they have responded to changing circumstances.

Ever since man began to live in nucleated rural communities there have always been some which have periodically failed completely. There are deserted villages which date from prehistoric times and others which have been abandoned within living memory. Some have been refounded, such as Cublington (Buckinghamshire), which was deserted in 1340 but repopulated again by 1410. Thousands of other villages have diminished in size without ever being completely deserted; these

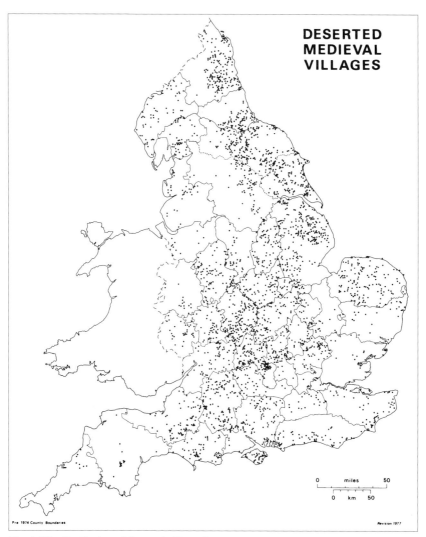

Fig. 1. The distribution of deserted villages in England (up to 1977). Many more have since been discovered.

fall into the category of shrunken villages.

In 1952 the newly established Deserted Medieval Village Research Group decided to distinguish between shrunken and deserted settlements according to the number of surviving houses. If there were fewer than three inhabited houses, the village was classified as being deserted: communities with more than three houses were merely *shrunken*. This is necessarily an artificial distinction as the same dynamic processes of settlement geography have been at work, whether a settlement has been completely or only partially abandoned.

Why study deserted villages?

A visit to the remains of a community which once thrived – a lonely farmhouse, isolated church or bumpy field – is in itself an evocative experience. Deserted villages frequently occupy attractive rural sites, making them intrinsically pleasant to study. We imagine the busy life of the village in its heyday and perhaps see, as Bishop Latimer recognised in his sermon to King Edward VI in 1549, that 'where there have been a great many householders and inhabitants there is now but a shepherd and his dog'. In their turn the sheep may have long since disappeared and modern agricultural techniques reduced the village remains to nothing more than different coloured markings in the growing corn (cropmarks) (see plate 3). Other villages may be truly 'lost' and no trace of them visible on the surface at all. Apart from the aesthetic pleasures of studying deserted villages, they provide important evidence for various disciplines at a variety of levels.

To the economic historian, historical geographer and archaeologist, deserted villages have immense value as reservoirs of information: they provide a window into history, uncluttered by later buildings and developments, and enable us to obtain a glimpse of a settlement as it was at the time it was deserted. Deserted villages preserve contemporary patterns of occupation, topography and buildings. They also help us interpret the population size and structure of former settlements as well as revealing something about their economy and everyday life. In many cases we are able to discover the reason why they were abandoned. They also help the historical geographer to reconstruct former patterns of settlement and land use and thus provide a barometer for economic historians to measure more general economic and social changes, reflecting, for example, the development of the late medieval English textile industry. Deserted villages are repositories of archaeological information, telling us about the nature of the world in which they existed and about the landscape around us today.

The sites of deserted villages are still being found, but they are also still being lost as the landscape adapts to changing economic pressures.

Plate 1. The borough of Caus, Shropshire, a failed medieval town – the wooded area covers a massive Norman castle. The town declined along with its strategic function in the late Middle Ages. There is now a single farm here.

For instance an analysis of deserted villages in Herefordshire recorded on aerial photographs taken in the 1960s showed that 75 per cent of them had earthworks that had been damaged or completely removed by 1980, largely as a result of intensive agriculture. Although there has been a major shift in the 1990s towards more environmentally friendly farming, sites continue to be damaged or lost through development pressures. All sites also suffer from natural ongoing processes of decay and destruction and there is still a need to locate and record any where field evidence survives.

2
When and why were villages deserted?

Early villages

The remains of early settlements dating from around 2000 BC onwards have been found in upland parts of Britain. Typical features include the footings of round houses, with associated small rectangular fields and heaps of stones piled up to enable land to be cultivated. Each of the round houses would have provided a home for an extended family.

By around AD 1000, round houses seem to have given way throughout mainland Britain to straight-sided ones. By this time, too, a reorganisation of the rural landscape had begun. Larger villages and market towns were being established to join, and sometimes replace, the existing pattern of small hamlets. These changes coincide with wider social, political and economic changes, including the development of feudal lordships, trading networks and parish churches. However, 'There was probably never a decade in the Middle Ages which did not see the death of one or more English village. A village was as mortal as a man.' (Beresford, 1954)

Beyond Domesday: Anglo-Saxon and Norman village desertions

The first accurate national census in Britain was not taken until 1801; it is therefore possible only to estimate the total population before this. Nevertheless, for England at least, documentary sources and the archaeological record do enable us to identify general demographic trends. A population decline in the late Roman and post-Roman period appears to have been followed by steady growth from about AD 700 to 1300.

Despite this growth, over one hundred abandoned Anglo-Saxon settlements have been located. For example, the village of West Stow (Suffolk) was quite suddenly, though apparently peacefully, deserted in the mid seventh century after being occupied for about 250 years. Many villages underwent major change of plan or location, leaving evidence of their migration and mutation. North Elmham (Norfolk), for example, was completely redesigned several times before its final desertion in the early twelfth century. Excavations at Maxey (Cambridgeshire), Sutton Courtenay (Oxfordshire) and St Neots (Cambridgeshire) have also demonstrated that there was a continual change of layout. The reasons for such alterations are not yet fully understood. Such early desertions rarely appear in the fragmentary surviving documentary records but they can be studied by archaeologists, who often locate these sites by accident, frequently as a result of redevelopment, such as village

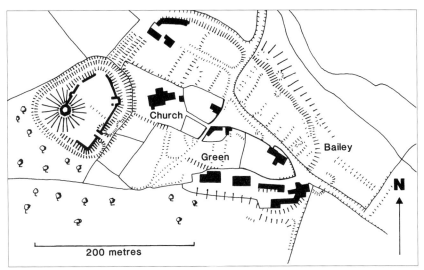

Fig. 2. Richard's Castle, Herefordshire. The earthworks of the deserted medieval borough: traces of the regular burgage plots and a central green can be seen in the large town bailey.

expansion or road construction.

The first reference to most English villages is in the Domesday Book. In this great survey of William the Conqueror's new kingdom, conducted in 1086, we are able to obtain some hints and references to the process of settlement abandonment in the eleventh century. For example, over a third of the places listed in Yorkshire and almost all those of Lancashire were listed as wholly or partially waste. Years of raids by Scandinavian armies and pirates must have taken a heavy toll, but much destruction seems to have been the result of William's terrible 'harrying of the North' between 1069 and 1070. Nevertheless, most of these places were eventually repopulated.

Permanent desertions because of war or pillage were relatively rare in England – sheer pressure of population meant that villages which were violently destroyed were normally soon re-established. Sometimes these new villages were laid out in a regular form such as East Witton (North Yorkshire). The Domesday Book demonstrates that there were some permanent desertions: several villages were cleared to make way for the King's hunting areas in the New Forest (Hampshire), while other Norman lords destroyed Saxon houses to build their castles. At Norwich, for instance, 113 houses were destroyed. Excavation at Oxford and at several other centres has revealed Saxon houses sealed beneath castle earthworks: at Eaton Socon (Cambridgeshire) excavations have shown that the twelfth-century castle overlay the whole village including the church.

In other circumstances the building of a castle could encourage settlement growth. There are many instances in the Welsh borderland of small towns and villages created within the shadow of Marcher lords' castles (plate 1). These castles and their associated settlements tended to decline when the border troubles subsided, making the castle's protection and the strategic siting of the settlement superfluous (fig. 2).

Expansion 1100–1300

During the twelfth century there were important developments in the landscape. Population pressure was the most important and resulted in the creation of many new towns and villages and the expansion of existing settlements throughout Britain. At the same time, the foundation of the great Cistercian abbeys and other religious houses reflected the emergence of the church as a powerful economic and political force.

From about 1100 to 1250, wasteland and the surviving woodland were being cleared: contemporary documents consistently record *assarts* or clearings in waste and wood. In an attempt to feed the growing numbers of people the limits of cultivation were being pushed as far as possible into marginal land. This process has been dramatically demonstrated by aerial photographs, which have located traces of medieval farming high above the present level of cultivation, for example in the Pennines and on Dartmoor (plate 2).

Growth continued until the late thirteenth century and is reflected in large numbers of new *boroughs*, established by the Crown, civil lords and church authorities. In Staffordshire, for example, only three boroughs were recorded in 1086 but by 1399 there were twenty-two. In Devon, the number rose from five in 1086 to eighteen by 1238. This pattern is repeated in many areas of Scotland (*burghs*) and can be traced elsewhere in Britain. These new creations experienced a variable rate of success. For instance, about half of Devon's boroughs, most of which were founded during this period, failed to survive in the long term. Some of these new boroughs were based on existing villages such as Cestersover (Warwickshire) (plate 3, fig. 3), which was granted market rights in 1257 but was subsequently abandoned; a series of plots can still be seen in the form of earthworks laid out at right angles to the main village street.

Monasteries were engaged in draining fens and reclaiming heaths and moorland, partly because they had the resources to do so, and also because much of the land granted to them was of marginal quality. The Cistercian rule insisted on solitude for the monks, and in the increasingly crowded twelfth-century villages sometimes had to be removed to enable abbeys to be founded. As the contemporary critic Walter Map wrote: 'you could say "grass grows green where Troy town stood". They create a solitude that they may be solitaries' (Allison, 1970). The monks' ledger-book for Stoneleigh Abbey records that they: 'settled in the place where Coulefield Grange now is, having moved away those who

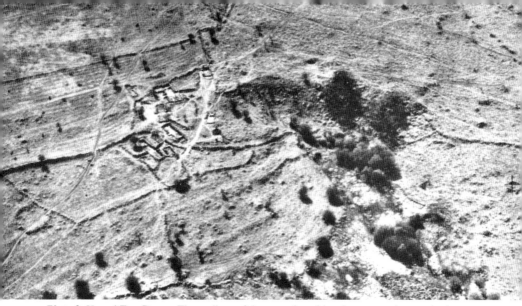

Plate 2. Hound Tor, Devon. The outlines of the stone-based longhouses can be seen in the centre of the aerial photograph. Traces of former field systems can be seen in the surrounding area.

Plate 3. Cestersover, Warwickshire. The ploughed-out remains of the deserted settlement can now be seen in the form of cropmarks (compare fig. 3).

lived there to the village now called Hurste' (Beresford, 1954).

Revesby Abbey (Northamptonshire) was given all the land in the three villages of Revesby, Thoresby and Stichesby by the Earl of Lincoln on its foundation in 1142. The Earl's charter confirms that seven peasants have taken land in exchange and thirty-one accepted their freedom – possibly by moving to a nearby town. When Byland Abbey (North Yorkshire) was founded close to Rievaulx, the villagers were moved to a new site some distance away, confusingly now called Old Byland. The original village probably stood just south of what is now Tile House Farm, but the monks soon discovered that their bells were too close to those of Rievaulx Abbey, with whom they soon found themselves in a campanological competition. Byland Abbey itself was moved to its present position 4 miles (6.4 km) away, and in time New Byland village grew up beside the new buildings.

Setback and decline

About 1250–1300, when the population of England had reached a peak of between three and five million, it began to decline. Various explanations have been offered for this reverse, the most plausible being that the population had simply passed the limit to which it could grow, given the economy, technology and agriculture of the time. Disease and soil exhaustion then became factors in reducing population. The tax assessments known as the Inquisitions of the Ninth, of 1341–2, recorded soil infertility and bad weather as reasons why the taxation liability of villages should be reduced. At Cuxham (Oxfordshire) wheat which had yielded a splendid 8.3 to every one quarter sown in 1288–99 was only yielding half as much fifty years later. Harvests failed in 1315, 1316 and 1321, and terrible sheep and cattle murrains occurred in 1313–17 and 1319–21 respectively. Storms on the coasts removed thousands of acres of agricultural land in Cambridgeshire, Kent and Sussex; while on the Scottish/English border raiding destroyed villages on both sides: the Scots destroyed about 140 Yorkshire villages in 1218. Some of these settlements, such as Mortham (North Yorkshire), were burnt in 1346 and were never rebuilt. None of these factors can fully explain the fall in population by itself; but certainly decline had already set in when at the end of June 1348 a ship docked at Melcombe Regis (Dorset) bringing with it the Black Death.

Conventionally the Black Death has been blamed for the dramatic reduction in the population in the years 1349–51, but few villages were totally and permanently deserted for that reason alone. Good farming land which had been abandoned soon attracted fresh settlers, as at Clothall (Hertfordshire). However, we should not underestimate its impact. Standelf, Tusmore and Tilgarsley in Oxfordshire were totally wiped out

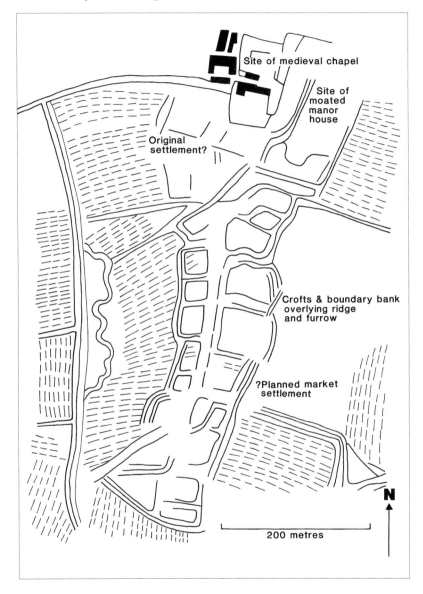

Site of medieval chapel

Site of moated manor house

Original settlement?

Crofts & boundary bank overlying ridge and furrow

?Planned market settlement

N

200 metres

Fig. 3. Cestersover, Warwickshire. Diagrammatic plan of the deserted village taken from an aerial photograph, showing the extension of the village over areas of former arable, which shows as medieval ridge and furrow.

and the records of the institutions of clergy for 1348–9 tell a grim story: at Winterbourne Clenston (Dorset) four successive rectors were appointed to the living and many other villages received two or more new parish priests over a period of a year or so. In some dioceses, as many as 60 per cent of the clergy died of the plague. The plague served to accelerate decline and the overall long-term effect was devastating, especially as the disease then became endemic for centuries.

At this time, too, a number of the boroughs founded with such enthusiasm before 1250 began to fail, as did several of the poorer and smaller villages which had been established on unpromising land under population pressure during the twelfth century. Thrislington (County Durham), for example, declined over a long period until one farm was able to take over all the land. As tenancies became vacant and labour scarcer, small farmers were able to take advantage of the situation: they moved from marginal lands to better soils, amalgamated holdings and took long leases on more favourable terms. Villages whose lands were poorest or where the terms on which land was held were unattractive shrank in size. Fordington (Lincolnshire), for example, had so few parishioners by 1450 that the parish was amalgamated with neighbouring Ulceby. At the bleak marginal site of Cold Weston in south Shropshire the settlement was in a decline before the Black Death; in 1341 the parish was assessed at 4s 8d compared with £5 3s in 1291. The assessors stated that there 'had once been abundance of cattle here', but that they had decreased in number because of the murrain which had hit the region. The account continues: 'the chapel is in a waste place and the living had been presented to four parsons within the year but none of them would stay, and there are only two tenants living by great labour and want, and others have absconded.'

Monasteries and colleges were among those landlords who found it increasingly hard to attract tenants. At Ibstone, on the Chilterns, a windmill constructed at some expense by Merton College, Oxford, in the 1290s lay derelict by 1330 through a lack of tenant farmers who needed to grind their corn there. At Upton (Gloucestershire) the Bishop of Worcester was unable to find tenants for his arable land, so he turned it over to sheep grazing (see plate 11); and at Wollashill (Worcestershire) a similar process occurred. As Professor Beresford remarks: 'The natural residual crop on land which had been abandoned was grass, so long as you had enough animals to keep the scrub from encroaching' (Beresford, 1954).

Pastures and profits

'Till now I thought the proverb did but jest which said a black sheep was a biting beast' (Thomas Bastard, *Epigrams*, c.1600). As the wool industry developed it became more profitable. In west and south-west

Plate 4. Fawsley, Northamptonshire. The church stands isolated in the grounds of Fawsley House, built by the Knightley family, who were responsible for depopulating the village for sheep pasture in the fifteenth century.

England pasture had always been important, while in Kent and Essex there had long been a mixed economy. In the midland counties of Oxfordshire, Northamptonshire and Leicestershire, however, much good arable land was now converted to excellent pasture. Landlords began to build up their flocks in a more determined fashion and it became worthwhile to remove villages, particularly those already in decline. Sheep rearing required much less labour than arable husbandry, and after desertion even the village sites themselves could be used for grazing (plate 4).

Most deserted village sites in England date from the period of the greatest prosperity of the wool trade in the fifteenth century, though depopulation for pasture continued well into the late Tudor period. The peak of desertion came at different times in different parts of the country, with the Midlands generally much earlier than the North. As the fifteenth century progressed the government began to take an interest in events. There were constant complaints from evicted tenants, and the evidence of ruined villages all over England was there for all to see. The depopulating landlords became a scapegoat for social and economic problems and were a popular target for contemporary pamphleteers and even dramatists:

'I can compare our rich misers to nothing so fitly as a whale. A' plays and tumbles, driving the poor fry before him, and at least devours them all at a mouthful; such whales have I heard on i' the land, who never leave gaping till they've swallowed the whole parish, church, steeple, bells and all.' (*Pericles, Prince of Tyre,* Act 2)

Yet all sections of society, even the more prosperous small farmers, were turning to sheep farming and, of course, more villages survived than were totally depopulated. Nevertheless, while a statute of 1402 declared that the monks and other subjects of the king should not be insulted by being called '*depopulatores agrum*' (depopulators of the fields), an Act of 1489 made it an offence to convert open fields to pasture if it involved the removal of smallholdings over 20 acres (8.1 hectares). Overlords were expected to take action to ensure that, in proven cases, arable holdings were reinstated. The preamble to the 1489 Act describes why the government was concerned:

'Great inconveniences daily doth increase by desolation and pulling down and wilfull waste of houses and Towns within that his (i.e. the king's) realm, and laying to pasture lands which customarily have been used in tillage, whereby idleness – ground and beginning of all mischiefs – daily doth increase, for where in some Towns two hundred persons were occupied and lived by their lawful labours, now be there occupied 2 or 3 herdmen and the residue fallen in idleness; the husbandry, which is one of the greatest commodities of the realm, is greatly decayed; churches destroyed; the service of God withdrawn; the bodies there buried not prayed for; the patron and curate wronged; the defence of this land against our enemies outwards feebled and impaired: to the great displeasure of God, to the subversion of the policy and good rule of this land.'

This polemic probably overstates the case but it is no accident that, during the sixteenth century, the landless peasant or vagrant becomes a common character in political tracts. The same century also saw the development of 'squatting' by landless peasants on the edges of common waste on a large scale. Contemporary writers make it clear that this was a classic conflict between private profit and social welfare – the interests of the overlords coincided with those of the depopulator and the grazier.

Nothing was done until a new Act against village depopulation was passed in 1515, followed in 1517 and 1518 by Cardinal Wolsey's Commissions of Inquiry to enforce the legislation. Although we cannot take all the evidence literally, these enquiries provide us with interesting insights into the depopulating process. For instance, it was reported that the Prior of Bicester had held five houses with 30 acres (12.1 hectares) attached to each and 200 acres (80.9 hectares) of his own at Wretchwick (Oxfordshire).

> 'He held this land on the second of March 1489 when those messuages were laid waste and thrown down, and lands formerly used for arable he turned over to pasture for animals, so three ploughs are now out of use there, and eighteen people who used to work on that land and earn their living there and who dwelled in the houses have gone away to take to the roads in their misery, and to seek their bread elsewhere and so are led into idleness.'

Not all those who dwelled in the houses can have been as poor as this statement would suggest. Wretchwick rentals for 1432–7 give the tenants' names, their holdings, and those holdings which were vacant. About a dozen families lived there, several of whom farmed extra holdings for which the priory could not find tenants, and some of these families, at least, are likely to have accumulated enough movable capital and expertise to start again elsewhere. The site can be clearly seen today as earthworks and banks surrounding the aptly named Middle Wretchwick Farm.

Privacy and pride: the creation of parks
It has been estimated that, by 1500, there were three times as many sheep as humans in England. However, from the mid fifteenth century the population had once more begun to increase. The profit motive still dominated the removal of villages but, already, this was being augmented by social factors as the status-conscious began to build exclusive parks for themselves, often incorporating landscaped gardens. As early as 1421 Henry V's brother, the Duke of Bedford, removed Fulbrook (Warwickshire) to make way for a park, while in 1440 a licence was granted to empark 200 acres (80.9 hectares) at Pendley (Hertfordshire), where a sizable village was removed. In 1503 a Scottish Act of Parliament required lords to construct parks, to include 'at least 1 acre of wood where there is no great woods nor forests'.

Such early parks had aesthetic and social overtones quite apart from the economic importance of their timber, grazing and game. Their development mirrors that of the country houses with which they were associated, and over the next three centuries park and house became larger and increasingly concerned with aesthetics and extravagance (plate 5). Emparking reached its zenith in the eighteenth century, when the removal of villages to create or enlarge parks was a widespread

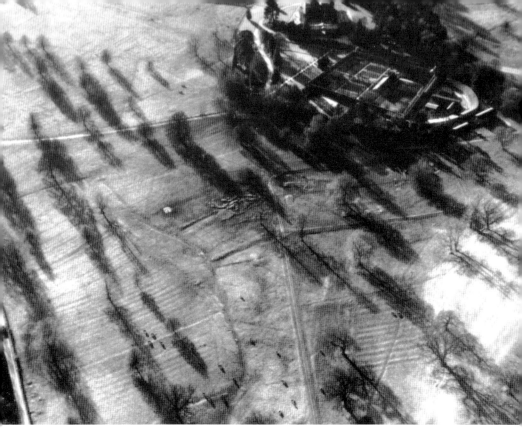

Plate 5. Berrington Park, Herefordshire. Traces of the fields of the former settlement can be seen within the great park of Berrington House.

phenomenon. Ickworth (Suffolk), Pudding Norton (Norfolk), Wimpole (Cambridgeshire) and other examples supplement Goldsmith's Auburn, identified above with Nuneham Courtenay (Oxfordshire), where:

'The man of wealth and pride
Takes up a space that many poor supplied;
Space for his lake, his park's extended bounds
Space for his horses, equipage and hounds.'
(The Deserted Village, 1770.)

In other places, the removal of villages and the creation of country houses, parks and gardens occurred together. In the celebrated case of Milton Abbas (Dorset) an entire market town was removed over a period of fifteen years by the first Baron Milton in order to construct his park. In 1673 there had been one hundred houses there, which he replaced with the small, regularly planned estate village. Such model or estate villages were designed to lie out of sight of the great houses and are usually recognisable by their neatly ordered, often identically designed houses, anticipating more recent suburban developments.

This process is well illustrated at Middleton Stoney (Oxfordshire), where a normal open-field village had been enclosed by agreement between the freehold farmers in 1698. During the following century and a quarter the Earls of Jersey, using a small medieval deer park as a base, gradually bought out the freeholders and extended their park until 1825, when the Oxford to Northampton road was diverted from its old route through the village to its present location on the edge of the park. The old village was destroyed and a new village built along the line of the new road (fig. 4). Other examples of this process can be seen at Wimpole (Cambridgeshire) and at Holkham and Houghton in Norfolk; Horninghold (Leicestershire) is an early twentieth-century example.

The creators of parks did not always trouble to rehouse displaced

Fig. 4. Middleton Stoney, Oxfordshire. Plan showing how the park was extended from its original small medieval nucleus to its present size and displaced the village in the process.

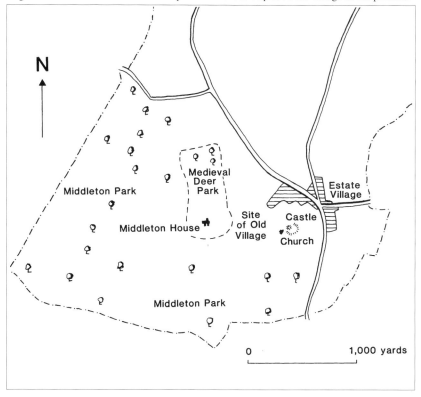

villagers; Stowe and Wotton Underwood (Buckinghamshire), for instance, disappeared altogether. At Hinderskelfe (North Yorkshire), where the Earl of Carlisle constructed Castle Howard, even the church vanished beneath the formal gardens and was not replaced. This practice was criticised by the landscape architect Humphry Repton:

> 'I have, on several occasions, ventured to condemn as false taste that fatal rage for destroying villages or depopulating a country, under the idea of its being necessary to the importance of a mansion ... As a number of labourers constitutes one of the requisites of grandeur, comfortable habitations for its poor dependants ought to be provided' (Beresford and Hurst, 1971).

Building a new country house did not necessarily mean the complete removal of a village, however. In some instances the village had already gone, providing an attractive vacant space for a house and park. A good example of this can be seen at Compton Wynyates (Warwickshire), where one of the earliest surviving country houses was built in about 1520 next to the isolated church of the already deserted village. The same process can be seen at Compton Verney (Warwickshire), where the village was abandoned several hundred years before the house was built.

Agricultural improvement

In the late eighteenth and in the nineteenth century, many lords did not confine themselves to making parks but engaged in a much wider reorganisation of the landscape. In England, Acts of Parliament were obtained to enclose strip fields, common grazings, heaths and moors, and to create new farms surrounded by hedged fields set out by land surveyors. Many village houses were subdivided for use by labourers but the settlements themselves survived.

In much of Scotland and northern Ireland, enclosure was a more gradual but more drastic process. Separate Acts of Parliament were not needed here, so major landowners were freer to reorganise their estates. The old pattern of agricultural hamlets (called *fermtouns* or *clachans*) was destroyed and replaced with new settlements and farmsteads as can be seen in fig. 5.

In the Scottish highlands, descendants of the sheep that had displaced English villagers in the fifteenth and sixteenth centuries now made their appearance. Landowners were faced with a rising population which could not be sustained by traditional agriculture. They could also see a

Fig. 5. (opposite). Agricultural improvements before (above) and after (below) on an estate near Kilmarnock. (After R. Millman.)

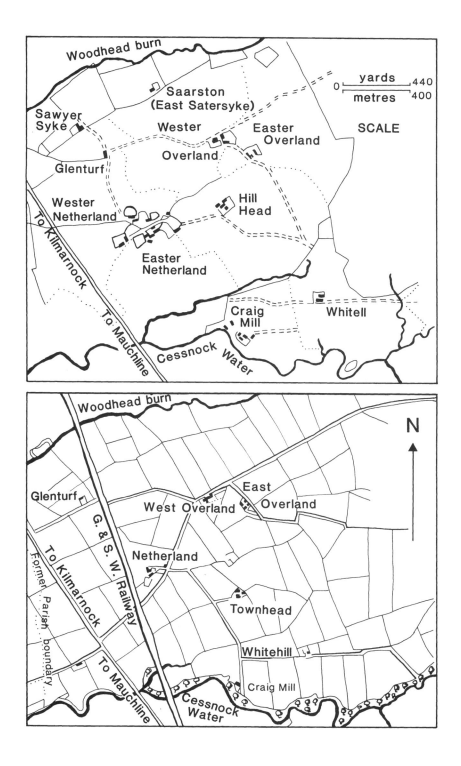

Top map labels:

Woodhead burn

Saarston
(East Satersyke)

Sawyer
Syke

Wester   Easter
Overland   Overland

Glenturf

Wester
Netherland

Hill
Head

Easter
Netherland

Craig
Mill   Whitell

Cessnock   Water

To Kilmarnock

To Mauchline

yards   440
0
metres   400

SCALE

Bottom map labels:

Woodhead burn

N

Glenturf

West Overland   East Overland

Netherland

Townhead

Whitehill

Craig Mill

Cessnock
Water

G. & S. W. Railway

To Kilmarnock

To Mauchline

Former Parish boundary

Plate 6. Newbold Grounds, Northamptonshire. Earthworks of a 'classic' deserted medieval village. The house platforms, sunken ways and precinct boundary can be clearly seen. The village is surrounded by ridge and furrow and seems in part, at least, to overlie former ridges.

ready market for wool in the mills of the industrial revolution. Whole communities were forcibly cleared from their homes and farms. Some moved to new crofting or fishing villages near the coast; others emigrated to Canada or Australia.

In many parts of Ross and Cromarty and Sutherland, the Clearances were so extensive that it is now difficult to trace the history of these deserted villages. Where they have been studied, for example at Rosal (Sutherland), settlement appears to have been continuous from at least the thirteenth century until 1814–18, when it was cleared along with all its neighbouring villages. Not all these settlements were small: many were as large as their English equivalents.

Ironically, at the time that the Clearances were under way, Queen Victoria was writing enthusiastically in *Highland Journals* that:

Plate 7. Newbold Grounds after ploughing. The site has been reduced to an irregular pattern of cropmarks which reflect the most deeply engraved features of the former site.

'this solitude, the romance and wild loveliness of everything here, the absence of hotels and beggars, the independent simple people, who all speak Gaelic here, all make beloved Scotland the proudest, finest country in the world.'
(*Highland Journals*, Thursday, 2nd September 1869)

Other reasons for desertion

There are many examples of settlements destroyed by natural agents and not rebuilt. Fire accidentally but permanently destroyed Bywell on Tyne in 1285, and the sea has removed villages from many parts of the coastline. At Hallsands (Devon) the sea was helped by the deliberate removal and sale of a protective shingle bank at the end of the nineteenth century. Now only a few ruins remain, perched on the cliffs. The coast of Holderness (East Yorkshire) has eroded by over a mile since Roman times and continues to lose about 3 feet (1 metre) a year. Likewise, in East Anglia a number of villages have been lost to the sea.

Large-scale mineral working has also been responsible for much destruction of deserted settlements. At West Whelpington (Northumberland), for example, a settlement which was not finally depopulated until about 1720 has been gradually destroyed as the hill on which it sits has been quarried away. Similarly, parts of the remains of the Anglo-Saxon deserted settlement complex at Catholme (Staffordshire) have disappeared as a consequence of gravel working. Numerous settlements of all periods have been destroyed since the 1960s on the sand and gravel terraces of the major river systems by a similar process. Urban sprawl has engulfed the sites of many former villages, both extant and deserted. St Pancras station in London, for instance, stands on the site of a former deserted medieval village.

Today villages in parts of Britain are still losing their populations at an alarming rate. More than a dozen have been totally deserted since the 1950s. Settlements established close to the mines and mills of the Industrial Revolution have declined with the industries they served. Until the 1970s the removal of redundant pit villages in County Durham was encouraged by Durham County Council, who demolished Leasingthorne, for instance, in 1969. Virtually all the seventy pits open in the county in the 1940s had been closed by 1990, and so the process of decline in industrial villages has been accelerated.

The mechanisation of agriculture has also depopulated villages: over 60 per cent of those people employed in farming in the 1940s have since left the land. Throughout Britain rural settlements have lost, on average, a third of their inhabitants as a result. Faxton (Northamptonshire) has been completely deserted since 1945. As shops and schools, bus services and post offices are withdrawn, further incentives are provided for people to move away.

Many more villages would be lying in ruins today were it not for the retired, the commuters and weekenders who occupy and maintain the houses in them; but such newcomers can do little to restore a disappearing way of life. They can even add to the problems of a village by forcing house prices out of the reach of local people and objecting to efforts to create local employment on aesthetic grounds. While the countryside is opened up to the car owner by an improved road network, this can also damage villages in unexpected ways. Eighteen months after the Brough bypass (Cumbria) was opened, employment in the village shops and hotels had dropped from 105 to 38. The village was not signposted from the new road and potential customers simply drove past.

Not all villages are left to the rich, the housebound and the elderly.

Imber (Wiltshire), for example, was taken over by the Army in 1943 to provide a training ground for street fighting, and the inhabitants were evicted. Even the name of the village has disappeared from the small-scale Ordnance Survey maps, although former villagers are allowed to visit the parish church, encased in a barbed-wire enclosure, once a year.

Paradoxically, many villages have disappeared not by the process of abandonment, but through expansion. Villages lying around the edges of large cities have been sucked into the spreading urban areas, while others lying further away have been drastically expanded as dormitory suburbs, so losing much of their original sense of community. Thus the process of rural settlement change continues at an increasing pace at the end of the twentieth century; but despite many vicissitudes the village remains an extraordinarily flexible and robust unit of human occupation.

3
What do deserted villages look like?

Villages deserted before AD 1300 have tended to leave little above-ground evidence. Early medieval peasant houses were generally built of wood, turf or unbaked clay and do not normally survive in earthwork form, although occasionally, where they have been ploughed out, they may be visible in the form of a cropmark. Most of the best-preserved Anglo-Saxon village remains have been found beneath later earthworks that have protected them from erosion, as at the castle site at Goltho (Lincolnshire), while the remains of West Stow (Suffolk) have been protected by a natural bank of sand, which was deposited over the site in the early medieval period. From the thirteenth century onwards some peasant houses were built in stone, leaving much more substantial remains. A significant proportion of deserted villages in England were abandoned in the later medieval period and the sites converted to permanent pasture. It is the surviving pasture sites, especially in the English Midlands, which provide the 'classic' form of earthwork deserted medieval village. Even where there are no earthworks, underlying buildings may reveal themselves in the form of *parchmarks*, which often describe the shapes of the houses very clearly, sometimes including interior divisions.

In the 1970s and 1980s there was a substantial ploughing-up campaign which resulted in the conversion of much former permanent pasture to arable and the consequent destruction of earthwork and parchmark sites. The results of such destruction can be seen in plates 6 and 7.

The creation of parkland was often responsible for the abandonment of villages but in some cases it resulted in the covering of the former village, or even town, remains with landscaping features; much of the original town of Milton Abbas (Dorset), for example, lies beneath an artificial lake. Nevertheless, a country house found in close association with a parish church and no surviving village is often a sure indication of former settlement abandonment and in such contexts earthworks are frequently found in close proximity to the house.

Where former settlements have been redeveloped or lost to natural erosion processes, there may be nothing now visible on the ground at all. However, sometimes urban open spaces can preserve evidence of deserted villages. Hilderthorpe (East Yorkshire), for example, lies on Bridlington's municipal golf course.

Isolated churches
The village church often survived when the village it served was

Plate 8. The isolated church of St Devereux, Herefordshire. The line of the village main street is today marked by a hollow-way.

abandoned (plates 8 and 9). This was not necessarily because churches were more solidly built than the surrounding houses, or for fear of divine retribution if they should be demolished, but because they belonged to a large independent organisation with its own rights, records and revenues. The church had a vested interest in the tithes and dues from a parish, as demonstrated during the Kiplingcotes enquiry (see page 5). Besides, parish churches could continue to serve nearby farms and hamlets long after the village was depopulated.

These now isolated churches can be seen all over England. East Anglia is particularly rich in such buildings: at Egmere (Norfolk), for example, the church was partly demolished in Henry VIII's time; close by there are two further ruined churches at Quarles and Waterden. In Devon, the dramatic impact of the isolated church at Brentor, with its associated earthworks, is strengthened by its imposing hilltop position.

In Scotland, religious changes since the Reformation have left most medieval parish churches in ruins. However, their ancient graveyards usually survive to suggest the former existence of a *kirktoun*.

Not every isolated church indicates the site of a deserted village, though. In Suffolk, for example, some may have been built as private chantries or chapels for the wealthy. Such was the origin of Gipping church, built by Sir James Tyrell in 1484–5, and there may be other reasons for a church now standing by itself. However, if you are just beginning to identify deserted villages, the isolated parish church or graveyard (of

Plate 9. Wolfhampcote and Braunstonbury (Warwickshire/Northamptonshire). Two deserted villages divided by a stream which forms the county boundary. The photograph incorporates all the characteristic features of the 'classic' earthwork deserted villages: an isolated church, village earthworks, a moated site, fishponds and ridge and furrow.

antiquity) marked on the 1:50,000 Ordnance Survey maps is as good a starting place as any.

Earthworks

Earthworks in the form of banks and hollows, known affectionately as 'lumps and bumps', are the principal visible evidence for deserted villages. Such earthworks sometimes spread over several modern fields, and the clearest overall impression of what they represent is usually obtained from the air or from the ground plan of a survey.

The roadways leading to the site of an abandoned village are sometimes noticeably sunken below the surrounding fields and often lead into the former streets of the settlement. Erosion by animals and carts over many years combined with weather action to create these hollow-ways, which are a common feature of deserted village sites and of surviving ancient country roads in parts of Britain.

In stony areas raised mounds may indicate former house sites, although sometimes the stones from the walls have been deliberately 'robbed', tending to create a more complicated pattern of earthworks. In areas where turf, timber and clay were the principal building materials the house areas may not be significantly raised above the general ground level and in some cases actually appear as slight square or rectangular depressions (fig. 7).

The house areas will be surrounded by those of outbuildings and boundaries to yards and paddocks (*tofts* and *crofts*). The houses with their closes form the core of the village earthworks and are often surrounded by a boundary bank which divided the inhabited area from the fields. Property boundaries represent one of the most ancient man-made elements in the landscape, although those defining individual gardens and house sites were more likely to change. Boundaries are therefore likely to be much older than the house remains visible on the surface. Excavations at deserted village sites have shown that, within the tofts, houses could be rebuilt on several different alignments without altering the basic boundary arrangements.

Earthworks of manor houses can sometimes be detected in the village. These are frequently larger house areas and they can be surrounded by a distinctive demesne or precinct boundary cutting them off from the rest of the village. Sometimes, too, they can be moated and the moat ditch will often be the most prominent earthwork feature on the site (fig. 8). Attention should be paid to whether the moated site fits comfortably within the general village layout or whether it cuts across earlier features. In the latter case the moated site could represent a manor house or early country house built on the site of the deserted village. Churches and chapels can also be distinguished on some sites. These, too, tend to be larger rectangular buildings and traces of the churchyard boundary may be identifiable. The alignment of the church earthwork may also be at variance to the general grain of the site. At Old Chalford (Oxfordshire), for instance, a prominent earthwork at the west end of the earthworks of a village is the only one to lie on a strict east to west axis contrary to the local topography, and because of its slightly larger size it has been convincingly interpreted as a chapel (plate 10).

The earthworks of watermills can sometimes be identified in the form of prominent platforms surrounded by channels (normally now dry) close to a stream. Most villages possessed at least one watermill during the Middle Ages, although this often lay at some distance from the main nucleus of the settlement. Other earthworks associated with medieval water management are fish and mill ponds, established by monastic houses or lords of the manor. Often these will be found in close association with the mill site. They normally take the form of a series of large rectangular depressions with earthwork dams,

Deserted Villages

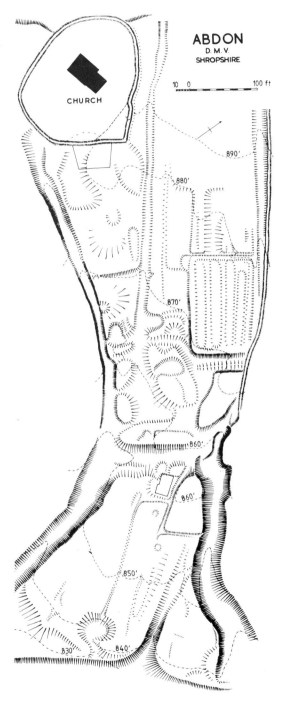

ABDON
D. M. V.
SHROPSHIRE

10 0   100 ft

CHURCH

890'

880'

870'

860'

860'

850'

830   840'

Fig. 6. Abdon. A hachured and contoured plan of a deserted village in south Shropshire.

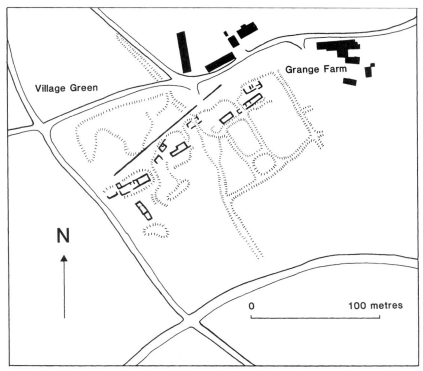

Fig. 7. Great Linford, Buckinghamshire. Plan showing the outline of excavated buildings in relationship to the above-ground earthwork features. (After Mynard.)

which have usually been breached. In some cases, however, such earthworks can be extremely complicated, involving the re-routing of long stretches of stream. Windmill mounds are also sometimes found, although normally they are located on the highest ground in the parish away from the village. These often have a large cross-shaped indentation in the top, where the base of the windmill stood.

Medieval fields

The most common of all earthworks associated with deserted villages, however, are the remains of agricultural activity, normally appearing as *ridge* and *furrow*. The highly characteristic corrugation can be located in many parts of Britain. A train journey through many areas of rural England, especially when the winter sun is low in the sky, will reveal, even to the casual observer, substantial areas of ridge and furrow. These earthworks are the remains of former open fields, which in medieval times formed much of the arable land. Most English villages had several of these large fields, subdivided into narrow strips, which were shared out among the villagers

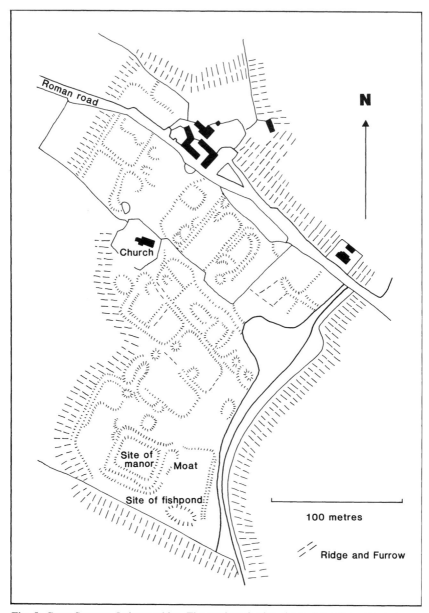

Fig. 8. Great Stretton, Leicestershire. The earthwork plan shows how the moated manor house fits into the general village layout.

(fig. 9). Bundles of strips made up *furlongs*, which were the basic unit of crop rotation, and often they ran up to the very precinct of the village.

Many different forms of strip fields existed throughout the British

Plate 10. Old Chalford, Oxfordshire. This photograph shows the remains of two settlements in the Glyme valley separated by a block of strip lynchets. On the centre left of the picture a rectangular structure lying at variance with the general pattern of earthworks apparently represents a former chapel.

Isles before the agricultural revolution of the eighteenth and nineteenth centuries. In parts of Ireland and western Scotland ridges were dug by hand and are therefore small and narrow. By contrast, in the English Midlands huge ridges were created by ox-drawn ploughs. Strip field systems were also dynamic and went through many changes over the centuries they were in use. Indeed they provide a study in themselves (see, for example, David Hall's *Medieval Fields* in this series).

Under the open-field system each villager was responsible for working his own strips, although a collective decision was needed to decide what crops should be grown and where. Each plough team worked up one side of the strip and back down the other, and the effect was always to pile the earth towards the middle, leaving hollows between the plots. If the end of open-field farming coincided with a change of land use to pasture, the shape of the strips was preserved. However, the ploughing-up campaign of the 1960s and 1970s has taken its toll and the quantity of ridge and furrow diminished annually until agricultural policy changed in the early 1990s.

In many parts of England, where landholding or farming arrangements

Fig. 9. Lower Heyford, Oxfordshire. Plan of the strip field system in 1604. The black strips are the parsonage holding and the dotted belong to a single farmer.

allowed, enclosure of strips was taking place by agreement from medieval times onwards. Where early enclosure took place and small bundles of strips were amalgamated, the pattern of the hedges will often reflect the characteristic reversed S of the original medieval plough line.

While early enclosures were usually small and irregular in shape, those made during the Agricultural Revolution of 1750–1850 required the re-planning of large areas. The English Enclosure Acts took the village fields as a whole and reallocated them in compact parcels of land. Sometimes the new boundaries followed those of the old system, but often they were laid out with no regard to the previous pattern. The centres of many villages declined at this time, as farmers built new houses out among the fields of their new holdings.

In Scotland and Ireland, powerful landed estates had no need to resort to Acts of Parliament to redraw the map. Old hamlets were demolished to make way for new farmsteads, set in rectangular fields (fig. 5). However, as in England, earlier features may survive to be discovered by the careful fieldworker.

When looking at the landscape it is important to try to establish the relationship between different features. For example, care should be taken to see if there are any traces of ridge and furrow underneath enclosures and house areas; this would indicate settlement expansion over former arable (see plate 6 and fig. 11). Conversely, in some cases it is quite clear that the settlement has contracted or shifted and that ridge and furrow have been laid out over the site of the former community (fig. 11). Earthwork boundaries of former fields are often to be found around the edge of the settlement area. These

Fig. 10. The plan of the clachan of Auchindrain, Argyll. (After RCAHMS.)

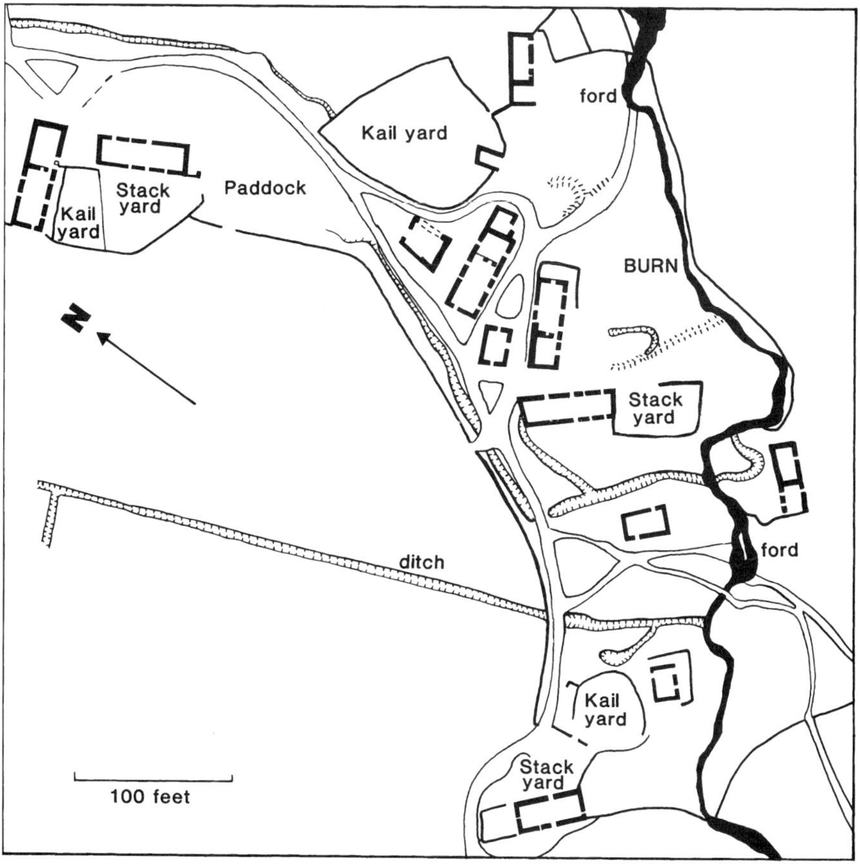

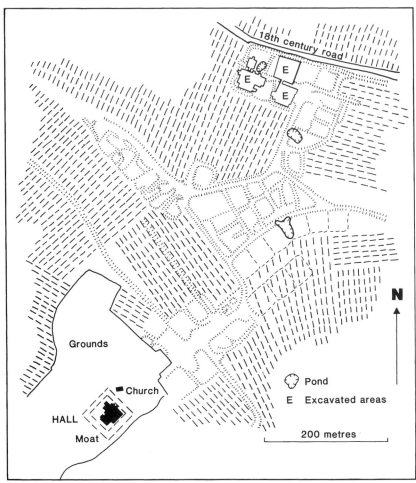

Fig. 11. Barton Blount, Derbyshire. An excavated site which has clear traces of ridge and furrow overlying former house areas (see plate 16). (After G. Beresford.)

enclosures sometimes take the shape of long rectangular blocks of land which acted as paddocks behind the garden area of the village, or they can be smallish square or rectangular enclosures representing early enclosure of the open-field system. It should be stressed, however, that the visible earthworks will reflect only the last phase of a village's development before desertion and generally give little indication of the complexity of archaeological features which lie beneath the surface (see fig. 7).

4
Archaeology and deserted villages

Deserted villages and the archaeologist

Until the middle of the twentieth century scholars of medieval history were largely concerned with great affairs of church and state and the magnificent monuments they produced; but since then increasing attention has been paid to the social and economic structure of society. One of the main areas of recent analysis has been the deserted village. The six hundredth anniversary of the Black Death in 1949 marked the beginning of an upsurge of interest in deserted villages. In studying the village we are examining a central element of the world that was lost with the Industrial Revolution – all the more fascinating because of its everyday ordinariness. Villages are able to bring us near to the lives of common people of past ages.

Archaeology has already made a significant contribution to our understanding of deserted villages. Although fewer than thirty excavations on deserted village sites took place between 1884 and 1952, an average of five a year were reported between 1953 and 1964, and some, mainly rescue, work has continued since then. Some digs have been carefully planned long-term projects, spread over several years, as at Hound Tor (Devon), Goltho (Lincolnshire) (fig. 12) and Upton (Gloucestershire) (plate 11), while at Wharram Percy (North Yorkshire) excavations took place every summer from 1950 to 1990 (fig. 13). Elsewhere emergency operations have been organised to salvage information within weeks or days as sites have been destroyed, but even hurried rescue projects are capable of producing important results.

It is important to examine the physical evidence of past communities in order to understand their layout, the nature of their buildings and how village topography developed and changed over the centuries. The analysis of documentary records provides evidence of the people who built, lived in and finally abandoned the villages. When historical, archaeological and ecological approaches are applied together village studies benefit considerably. Combined campaigns of investigation have paid rich dividends at sites such as Wharram Percy.

The contribution of archaeology: the living picture

It is not easy to obtain a clear picture of the earliest villages. Despite attempts to classify rural settlements according to their layout, there are almost as many categories of village forms as there are villages. Commonly the plan is linear, with one or two rows of houses laid out

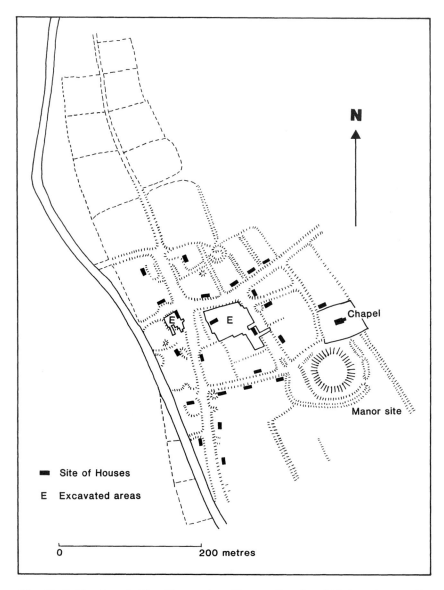

Fig. 12. Goltho, Lincolnshire. The regular village earthworks which have been partly excavated. Late Saxon houses have been found underneath the manor house site. (After G. Beresford.)

Plate 11. An early phase of the excavations at Upton, Gloucestershire, where the lower courses of a medieval longhouse have been uncovered.

along a central street; crossroad villages provide a variation on this theme (plate 12).

Another principal village form is based on the central green. This can be square, oval, rectangular or triangular, but in all cases the intention is the same – to provide a broad common open space in the heart of the community. The green had various uses, for instance for fairs and markets, for grazing village animals and to provide a meeting place for villagers (plate 13). Many villages were laid out around greens in the Middle Ages or later and do not owe their regular plans to Anglo-Saxon settlers as was previously thought. Indeed there are several instances where a village plan of apparent antiquity can be dated to the ambitious emparking schemes of an eighteenth- or nineteenth-century squire.

Villages derived from settlements with urban aspirations often have distinctive plans. A grid pattern of streets belonging to a planned medieval town which failed to prosper is visible at Newton (Isle of Wight). New market towns of the twelfth and thirteenth centuries were often designed with a series of long thin *burgage plots* facing a main street or market place and backing on to a *back lane*. This allowed the maximum number of tenants to be accommodated with a frontage well placed for the establishment of shops. Such features can still be seen in the arrangements of many surviving towns and villages which failed to develop beyond their original nuclei.

In Scotland and Ireland, rural settlements were generally smaller than in England, with no recognisable plan. In the typical *clachan* or hamlet, houses could be placed at various angles to each other, sometimes

Plate 12. An aerial photograph of the deserted village of Wharram Percy, North Yorkshire, seen under snow, which highlights the village features.

Fig. 13 (opposite). Wharram Percy. Excavations were carried out on this extensive earthwork site between 1950 and 1990. The work has shown that the medieval village must now be seen in a much broader chronological perspective, with some village boundaries originating in pre-Roman times. (After M. Beresford and J. G. Hurst.)

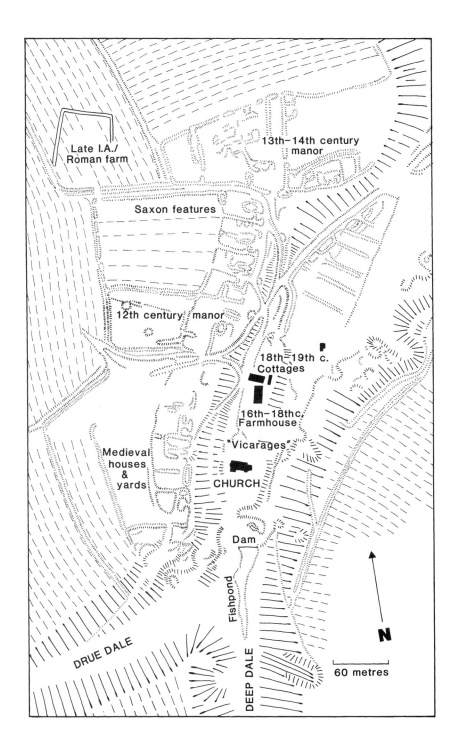

Late I.A./
Roman farm

13th–14th century
manor

Saxon features

12th century manor

18th–19th c.
Cottages

16th–18th c.
Farmhouse

"Vicarages"

Medieval
houses
&
yards

CHURCH

Dam

Fishpond

DRUE DALE

DEEP DALE

N

60 metres

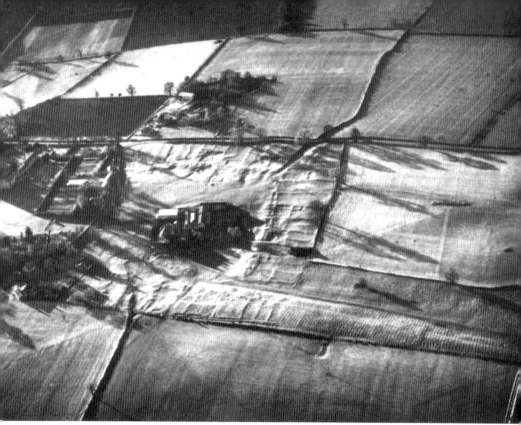

Plate 13. Walworth, County Durham. The earthworks of a deserted green village. House platforms and enclosures can be clearly seen lying around a square green now occupied by a farm and outbuildings. A country house and its gardens occupy the left-hand side of the old village.

around a central open space (fig. 10).

One of the most striking features of medieval rural settlement is the degree of change that took place within apparently rigid boundaries. Churches, manor houses, individual farmsteads and even whole villages were replanned and resited. An early village at Bardolfeston (Dorset) consisted of a series of rectangular crofts which probably contained timber buildings; but this was overlaid by a later arrangement comprising a single street with two rows of stone houses, on a totally different alignment. A similar radical realignment and rebuilding took place in the thirteenth century at the village of Seacourt, just outside Oxford, which was subsequently deserted.

Village houses

Since the mid 1950s archaeological investigation has enabled the identification of various categories of house plans from the Middle

Ages (fig. 14). At the simplest level there are one-roomed *cots*. They were heated by an open hearth, from which smoke escaped through a louvred or hipped roof. *Longhouses* or *laithe-houses* can be found in much of Britain from the thirteenth and fourteenth centuries (plate 14), although earlier examples have been found at Hound Tor (Devon) (see plate 2). These were divided into two sections, often by a cross passage between opposing doorways. One end was used as living accommodation for the family, while the other served either as a byre for animals or a store for farm products and equipment. Longhouses have been found throughout Britain and Ireland, and also on the European mainland (plate 14). Modified forms continued to be built in some areas until the

Fig. 14. English and Welsh medieval house types.

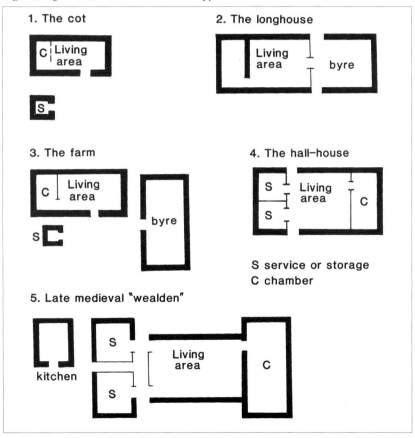

Plate 14. A longhouse still in occupation in Brittany. Animals live in the left-hand part of the building, while humans occupy the right-hand side.

nineteenth century and some are still occupied even today. The *black-houses* of the Western Isles of Scotland are an adaptation of the form to the local climate (fig. 15).

Hall-houses are closely related to longhouses. These were built by more prosperous yeoman farmers, especially in southern and midland England, in imitation of the houses of the wealthy. They had a main hall divided from the service and storage areas by a cross passage, while at the other end of the hall would be a series of smaller rooms, one of which would serve as a bedroom. All these categories shared a common format consisting of an open living area with a number of attached rooms. Large timber halls and barns were sometimes aisled in the same manner as churches.

The size and complexity of the medieval houses naturally reflected the wealth and status of the owners. Detached kitchens and storehouses were associated with early manor houses; and by the later medieval period courtyard farms (fig. 16) appear in a peasant context. There are a number of examples of longhouses being rebuilt in the form of courtyard farms at this time, such as at Gomeldon (Wiltshire) and Upton (Gloucestershire) (fig. 17).

Medieval houses revealed by excavation vary considerably in their plan, size and complexity. They show that the popular impression of medieval squalor is wrong; often the clay floors of peasant houses were

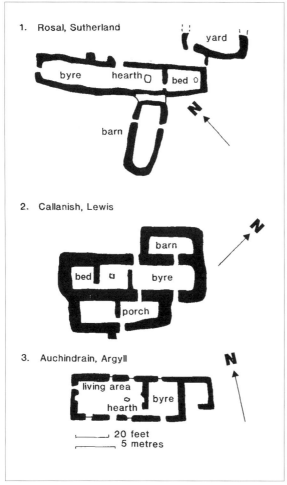

Fig. 15. Some Scottish rural house types. 1. A longhouse and barn from Rosal, Sutherland. 2. A Hebridean black-house from Callanish, Lewis. 3. A longhouse from Auchindrain, Argyll.

so thoroughly swept that hollows have been created which then had to be levelled up. Rubbish was largely organic and was therefore taken out and spread as fertiliser on the fields. Everything possible was recycled, including stone, turf, thatch and timber from houses themselves. This has left a complex, shallow stratigraphy on deserted village sites that can be difficult and time-consuming to unravel.

Pottery and other small finds

The excavation of deserted medieval village sites produces a broad range of articles, the most common and durable of which are pottery. The pottery types found in the village will reflect the period when the

Fig. 16. Caldecote, Hertfordshire. The excavated remains of an early farmyard complex. (After G. Beresford.)

village was occupied, its prosperity and the range of its trading contacts. Apart from the pottery, iron objects are sometimes found if soil conditions are favourable to their preservation. These include blades, nails, spikes, hinges, buckles and horseshoes, as well as padlocks and keys. Bells for animals and small personal ornaments made of copper or bronze, as well as lead weights, are also found.

Stone was used in medieval villages for mortars and querns; whetstones and spindle whorls have also been recovered. Bone objects recovered from sites include combs (often for weaving) and knife handles. Although glass was expensive and treated with great care in medieval times, occasionally glass from bottles, windows or beads is found. From the fourteenth century onwards bricks and tiles appear, especially in eastern England.

One significant fact to emerge from archaeological work on deserted villages is the relative absence of medieval coins. Whereas on most Romano-British sites coins tend to be plentiful, relatively few contemporary coins are found on deserted medieval villages, and this confirms that at a peasant level little cash was used. At Upton (Gloucestershire), for example, apart from a collection of Roman coins, five years of excavation produced only a single medieval farthing.

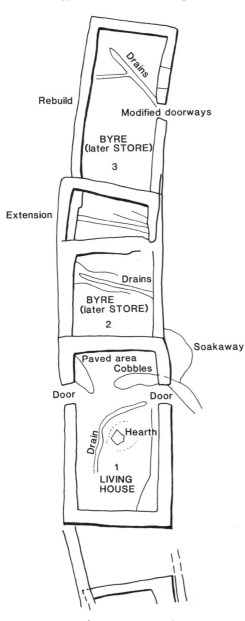

Fig. 17. Upton, Gloucestershire. The phases of development from a longhouse (1), to a building where the animals were segregated from the living quarter (2), to a separate farmyard and byre (3). (After P. Rahtz.)

Exchange and barter appear to have provided the main mechanisms of trade and some objects were obviously traded over considerable distances. At Wharram Percy, for example, sherds of pottery from the Netherlands, France and Germany have been found.

Environmental evidence

Traces of materials presumed to be perishable may survive even on sites which were deserted at an early date. Wood – so important to the pre-industrialised economy – can be preserved in either a waterlogged condition or in a charred condition as charcoal; and seeds can sometimes be recovered that will help to determine which crops were grown. Seeds and other environmental evidence also provide information on the general nature of past landscapes and climatic trends.

Molluscs, beetles and spiders provide information about the environment: some species prefer cool, wet, shady areas, while others prefer open ground. At Wharram Percy the snail shells found indicated open ground in the area of the site, with the presence of hedges and rough vegetation such as 'dank grass, patches of nettles and other tall herbs' (Hurst, 1979).

Animal bones indicate the relative importance of different species to farming in the village and help us understand the farming methods. At Upton (Gloucestershire) cattle apparently provided 53 per cent of the meat consumed from domestic stock and were mostly killed before they were three years old, while 97 per cent of the sheep lived beyond two years, suggesting that they were not kept primarily for meat but for their wool. Pigs provided only 3 per cent of domestic meat supplies. Medieval animals were much smaller in size than their modern counterparts. Cattle and sheep were apparently slaughtered at about two years, although some of the cattle lived to five years old, while pigs were generally killed at eighteen months. The evidence indicates that many more animals were overwintered than was previously thought, and we should treat the conventional idea of the wholesale slaughter of stock in the autumn with some caution. Nevertheless, animals were killed and eaten in considerable quantities, and the methods and techniques of butchery can be studied in the knife-cuts often visible in the bones. At Wharram Percy and other inland sites bones from sea fish were also found, which suggested that fish had been transported in a dried form from the coast, although freshwater fish and eels were frequently farmed locally in fishponds.

Human bones can reveal much about population structure, life expectancy and disease. Unbaptised infants were not buried in churchyards, and at Upton a child of three to six months was found buried under the floor of a house. Little comprehensive work has yet been published on excavated cemeteries from medieval village sites; but it should be possible in time to obtain from them a reasonably accurate picture of the size and age range of the village population, and this will, in turn, assist the interpretation of documentary records such as tax assessments.

The role of the amateur

Excavation of deserted villages is a complex business, and techniques have been developed by which large areas can be seen in plan and the maximum information retrieved. Untrained and inexperienced digging produces very little of value, and even a small hole or trench dug into a site can cause extensive and irreparable damage if not carried out by, or under the direction of, a qualified archaeologist. The techniques can be learned, but the only satisfactory way to do this is by gaining practical experience on archaeological sites. Some suggestions and addresses for those interested are given in chapter 8. Unsupervised excavation should not be undertaken in any circumstances.

Archaeological work is not all excavation, however. In recent years increasing attention has been paid to landscape survey and other non-destructive research, and this by itself produces important results. A sketch survey which shows the general layout of earthworks and other topographical features may be the only record made of a site before it is destroyed. The archaeologist and the historian also have much to offer one another, and a great deal of fascinating and valuable information can be extracted from documentary sources. Much can be learned harmlessly, an absorbing leisure interest developed and useful work done by the diligent part-timer.

5
How to discover deserted villages

As we have seen, many thousands of deserted settlements have been found in Britain. However, the inquisitive fieldworker should not be discouraged as there are undoubtedly many more to be located. Even where sites are known, we often have very little background information about them. In many cases, we only know that sites exist – even a basic survey has never been carried out.

Discovery in the field

Where there is reason to suspect the existence of deserted village sites, a comprehensive field survey can be undertaken to locate them. This can involve walking every field in a parish in order to identify areas of earthworks or, in ploughed areas, surface scatters of building stone, pottery, burnt clay and charcoal. Such concentrations of occupation debris are normally clearly visible for the first few years after an earthwork site has been ploughed.

Such field surveys should include the recording of ridge and furrow, either from ground observation or by extracting the information from aerial photographs. In some parts of England where ridge and furrow is very extensive it has been possible to locate former village sites by identifying the gaps in the ridge and furrow. A group of deserted villages in the area of Cestersover (Warwickshire) was found in this way (Baker and Harvey, 1973).

Discovery from secondary sources

The best starting point for anyone intent on discovering deserted villages is the local *Sites and Monuments Record* (SMR). These are maintained by, or on behalf of, local authorities throughout Britain and Ireland to provide a local source of information for planning and research. They include details of all recorded archaeological sites for their areas. Arrangements vary but the Council for British Archaeology (CBA) (see chapter 8) can provide details. Alternatively, local planning departments should be able to indicate the location of 'their' SMR. Some are much more detailed than others, depending on the resources made available to them. As well as these local records, National Monuments Records for England, Wales and Scotland are maintained in Swindon, Aberystwyth and Edinburgh respectively (see chapter 8 for addresses). Both local and national records can be consulted by appointment.

Local and national museums, libraries and records offices are also

Plate 15. Winterbourne Farrington, Dorset. Irregular earthworks of a deserted village are referred to in Thomas Hardy's *The Trumpet Major*, as is the gable end of a ruined church sitting in the middle of the photograph.

good sources of information. Most local authority library services maintain reference collections of local studies material, which can be useful, and archives or records offices can generally be relied upon to contain at least some old maps (see page 56). For many English counties the volumes of the *Victoria County History* are worth checking, particularly where studies have been produced in recent years.

In most parts of Britain there are local archaeological societies which produce journals and reports. Some of them maintain their own comprehensive reference libraries and even museums. The CBA can provide details of these.

Aerial photographs

The National Monuments Records, SMRs and most planning departments have good collections of aerial photographs. Aerial views have been instrumental in the discovery of a large number of deserted medieval village sites. Indeed many sites exist only on photograph as they have been destroyed since the photographic record was made. Sites are best viewed from the air, where the earthworks of a deserted village, which on the ground apparently form a meaningless muddle,

Plate 16. Barton Blount, Derbyshire. The clearly defined earthworks of a strung-out deserted village, showing a wide variety of earthwork forms. The village has been excavated (see fig. 11).

fall into place, with a clear pattern of houses and streets (plate 15). Similarly, even on sites that have been ploughed it is often possible to identify scatters of stone, tile and other occupation debris, which through different colours and textures describe the pattern of former settlement. In some cases the sites will show as cropmarks, that is, differential growth in a crop indicating some of the more deeply engraved features of the former settlement. The aerial photograph is particularly valuable in showing the site in its context, notably in its relationship to the former and existing field patterns, and in identifying trackways and other associated features. In some cases it is possible to marry a photograph with a ground survey and thus enhance the amount and value of the survey (plate 16 and fig. 11).

The fieldworker should be aware of the purpose for which the photograph was taken. Many vertical aerial photographs have been taken for planning and other purposes and record archaeological material incidentally. Some of the best archaeological photographs are the oblique ones that have been taken by private individuals or by the Cambridge Committee for Aerial Photography or the National Monuments Records mentioned above. These organisations have extensive collections of archaeological aerial photographs and should be consulted by the serious field researcher.

Fieldwork

It is seldom possible to discover deserted villages by setting off at random into the countryside. Some preliminary detective work is necessary, and a good basis for this is the Ordnance Survey 1:50,000 map. A guide to former settlement patterns is provided by ancient parish churches. Isolated medieval churches or graveyards may indicate deserted village sites. They are not infallible clues, however, because often no church survives from a former settlement; in such cases a modern civil parish without a parish church may be equally indicative.

Apparently random junctions of footpaths and trackways in the middle of an uninhabited area will sometimes pinpoint an abandoned settlement. For example, the deserted village of Papley (Northamptonshire) was traced partly by the meeting place of four footpaths and two bridlepaths in a remote part of Warrington parish. The patterns of boundaries can also provide useful clues. The shape of a parish boundary may be significant. Where the main settlement has been deserted parishes have often been amalgamated with others, so that an unusual shape for the area is produced. West Halton parish (Lincolnshire) is shaped like an L which has fallen on its back. One arm represents the ancient parish of West Halton; the other is that of the deserted village of Haythby.

Further indications are provided by larger-scale maps, such as the 1:25,000 and 1:10,000 Ordnance Survey series. These show individual fields and can therefore help in locating land units and farm boundaries, features which helped to locate four deserted and shrunken villages in Charminster parish (Dorset). By comparison with other land units in the area it was possible to identify where settlements were likely to have been; a search on the ground then located them.

Patterns of field boundaries can also be significant. For example, small, irregular fields can sometimes be found well away from an existing settlement, which can sometimes help to locate a deserted village. Field boundaries can also continue the lines of roads which now stop abruptly for no apparent reason, because the villages to which they once led have gone.

Ordnance Survey maps at 1:50,000 and larger scales often mark earthworks and moats which can represent former villages and manor houses. The names of features on maps can help a great deal in the search for abandoned villages. An isolated farm may give its name to a whole parish, for example, suggesting the last vestiges of a once more important settlement. The names of the Oxfordshire deserted villages of Wretchwick and Whitehill are preserved in Middle Wretchwick Farm and Old Whitehill Farm, for example. Place-name evidence really comes into its own, however, when we turn from current to old maps.

Old maps

No comprehensive large-scale mapping of Britain as a whole was undertaken until the Ordnance Survey was established in the late eighteenth century. However, for some villages there are early estate plans, which normally incorporate valuable information (plate 17). One of 1583, for example, shows a plan of the already deserted village of Fallowfield (Northumberland) and a Leicestershire plan dated 1586 has the caption 'where the towne of Whateboroughe stood' (plate 18). Field names such as *Town Field*, *Town End* and *Township Field* can suggest a former village (as can corrupt forms of these names such as *Downship*). Empty plots of land at East Layton (County Durham) are marked as 'the scyte of the houses' on a plan of 1608. A *Millfield* is worth examining for traces of water channels or windmill mounds; *Blacklands* can refer to occupation debris which has discoloured the soil; similarly *Stonesfield*, away from existing settlement, provides a possible indication of a former community. Comprehensive collections of field names can often be found on nineteenth-century enclosure, tithe or estate maps.

A useful link between old and current maps is provided by the mid-nineteenth-century 1:10,560 (6 inch) first edition of the Ordnance Survey. These early surveys are now important historical documents in their own right: the sheets show many details and landmarks which can be traced on earlier maps but which have since disappeared.

Primary sources

Primary sources of information are contemporary references to sites when they were still occupied. These include estate and manor court records and surveys made by government, church and manor to assess taxes, rents and rates. Not all of these are as inaccessible as might be thought, although many can be viewed in county archives. Some collections of medieval documents have been transcribed and printed by county or national societies.

After 1801 the population census returns can be used to identify parishes with few inhabitants, and those of 1851 and 1861 recorded people's birthplace and occupation. Caution is needed in the use of census material, as a population of fifty in a parish could reflect the large number of servants and staff in a country house, where the village had long since disappeared. At Wharram Percy a population of 35 in

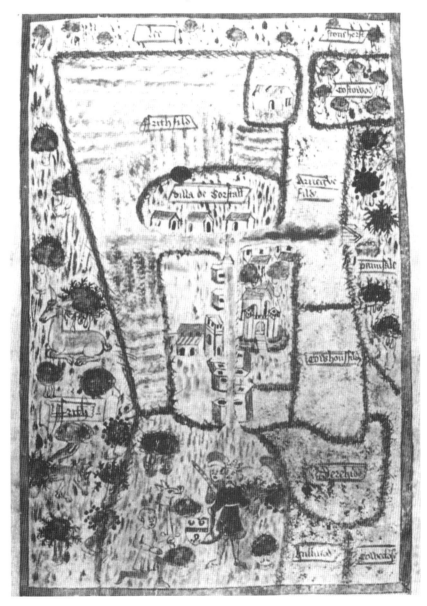

Plate 17. A plan of Boarstall, Buckinghamshire, dated 1444. It is one of the earliest surviving village plans and shows the church and moated site surrounded by houses and beyond that the village fields. The village has shrunk considerably since the map was drawn.

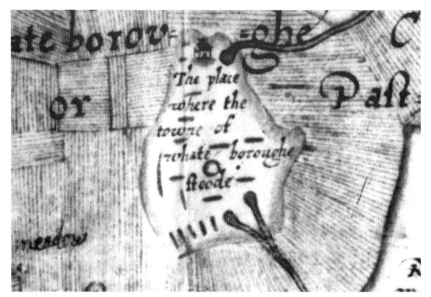

Plate 18. A plan of Whatborough, Leicestershire (1586), showing 'The place where the towne of Whateboroughe stood'. A single house sits on the village area which is surrounded by strips of the open-field system.

1841 became 171 ten years later: but this sudden influx of people lasted only as long as was necessary to build a nearby railway tunnel. After this the 'bricklayers', 'stonemasons' and 'miners' of 1851 moved on. The enumerators' returns for the 1851 census provide us with detailed information on the age, occupation and place of birth of all recorded persons.

Making a record
The other primary source of information is the site itself. Much can be learned if a careful record is made of a site, as the process of recording turns up many details which would otherwise be missed. A questionnaire has been produced by the Medieval Settlement Research Group to guide fieldworkers and is reproduced at the end of this book. Apart from attempting to discover the answers to the questions it contains, the researcher should try to make some sort of plan of the site, even if this is only a rough sketch.

The 1:10,000 (formerly 6 inch) Ordnance Survey maps can be used as a base on to which the overall extent of earthworks and ridge and furrow can be sketched, but for more detailed sketches a larger scale, such as 1:2,500, is required. Although a sketch plan can never be

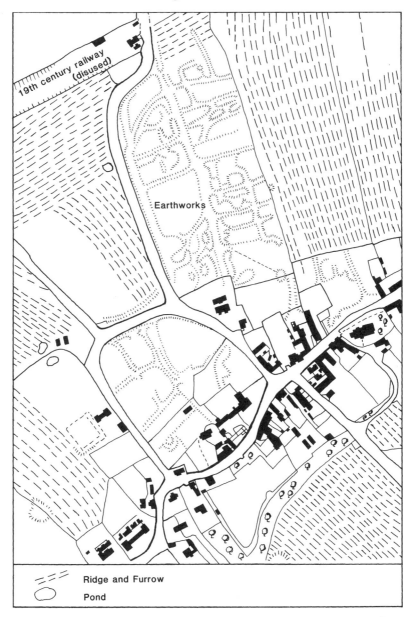

19th century railway (disused)

Earthworks

Ridge and Furrow

Pond

Fig. 18. Theddingworth, Leicestershire. An earthwork plan of the shifted medieval village. Compare with plate 19.

Plate 19. Theddingworth, Leicestershire. A shifted village (compare with fig. 18).

compared to a measured survey, it can be of great value and requires relatively little skill. Apparently meaningless mounds take on recognisable form; and if a site is subsequently destroyed the sketch may have to serve as the only record of the site (fig. 18 and plate 19).

The method by which a sketch survey is produced is fairly simple. It is advisable to record several identifiable fixed points, such as the corner of a building or a boundary line, which can be subsequently related to points on the map. The site should be thoroughly explored by walking all round it, and the largest and most obvious features recorded first. The less obvious details can then be filled in. Distances should be expressed in relative terms, such as 'half-way along hedge', although, if the fieldworker has a consistent step, pacing out distances makes drawing simpler and considerably more accurate. Further accuracy can be achieved by using a prismatic compass to record the bearings of each part of an earthwork site. Heights of earthworks need to be estimated, unless an instrument survey is undertaken, and it is normal practice to regard the overall ground surface as flat for this purpose. Slopes and banks are generally shown by hachures (or 'tadpoles', as they are called). If there is a level or theodolite available spot heights and contours can be added. Levels should be taken on the nearest benchmark to obtain absolute heights above sea level. Benchmarks are shown on 1:2,500 maps.

An alternative technique, more suited to smaller sites, involves the use of two or more 30 metre tapes and some garden canes or ranging poles. Here a straight base line is laid out across the middle of the site to be surveyed and measurements are taken off it at right angles. Although this should produce a fairly accurate survey, it is not generally clear where slopes begin and end, and for large areas a series of base lines will be needed with at least two people required to hold tapes and make notes. Scale plans can be made, depending on the detail required, at 1:2,500, 1:1,250 or even 1:500. There are also several other simple survey techniques which can be used. Details of these can be found in the fieldwork books suggested in Chapter 7.

Whatever sketches and field notes are made, it is essential to label them fully and include as much information as possible. The fieldwork questionnaire for deserted villages, reproduced at the end of the book, provides a good basis for notes. The scale of any drawing should be shown. The direction of north should be indicated, even if approximately, and some means of relating the site to the surrounding topography is very important. The name of the recorder should always be included.

Once a site has been discovered and recorded, no matter how roughly, it should be made known to the local authority archaeologist for inclusion in the Sites and Monuments Record (SMR). It will then be available to future researchers. Because SMRs are used to monitor development proposals, inclusion can also help to conserve sites for future enjoyment and study. All work done adds to our total knowledge of deserted villages, and some exceptional sites may warrant preservation as historic monuments.

6
Where are the deserted villages?

It would be impossible to list here all the thousands of deserted villages that have now been found in Britain and Ireland. Maurice Beresford and John Hurst published a gazetteer in their book *Deserted Medieval Villages* in 1971; and there is another in Richard Muir's *Lost Villages of Britain*, issued in 1982. The latter includes a note against each giving the reason for desertion where this is known. However, nearly all the sites in these gazetteers are on private land, and the permission of landowners and farmers is needed to visit them.

In recent years several local authorities have bought deserted village sites to conserve them. Somerset County Council, for example, has acquired **Nether Adber** and **Marston Magna**. Advice on visiting these and other sites should be sought from the local authority archaeologist. Planning departments can usually provide a telephone number.

As so many surviving villages have shrunk, moved or realigned themselves in the course of their history, it is often possible to see typical signs of desertion, like the earthworks of hollow-ways and house sites, around surviving villages or within landscape parks.

Some sites require no special arrangements to visit. A few examples follow, but this list is not exhaustive.

Auchindrain (Argyll) (fig. 10): good visible remains; illustrates the form of the traditional Scottish clachan. Finally abandoned in 1954, it is now a Folk Museum. (NN 032033.)

Birsay (Orkney): the outlines of Viking longhouses, a church and other buildings have been revealed by excavation. (HY 243284.)

Cosmeston (Glamorgan): a medieval village reconstructed on its original site, following excavation. (ST 176690.)

Heath (Shropshire): the extensive earthworks of the village surround an almost perfect Norman chapel. (SO 556856.)

Hound Tor (Dartmoor, Devon): an evocative site high on the moor, with longhouse foundations clearly visible. Now opened by Dartmoor National Park. (SX 745789.)

Jarlshof (Shetland): a long sequence of prehistoric, Viking and later settlement remains are visible, some standing to several metres high. It is one of the most dramatic archaeological sites in Europe. (HU 399069.)

Kilpeck (Herefordshire): a splendid Norman parish church and castle mound are adjacent to the earthworks of the former village, which in turn have a bank and ditch around them. (SO 445315.)

Porth-y-nant (Caernarvonshire): a nineteenth-century quarrying village, deserted during the 1950s. Reached by a steep zigzag path through forestry plantations. (SH 346445.)

Rosal (Sutherland): a victim of the Highland clearances in 1814–18, it has been opened to the public by the Forestry Commission, which now owns the site. (NC 688416.)

St Kilda (Scotland): the most remote deserted village in the British Isles, set out in the Atlantic, but a World Heritage Site. Its inhabitants were evacuated at their own request before the Second World War. Now owned by the National Trust for Scotland. (NF 103993.)

Tyneham (Dorset): taken over by the Army during the Second World War, it is now open to the public most weekends. The ruins of the houses have been conserved and there is an exhibition in the former village school. (SY 882803.)

West Stow (Suffolk): an Anglo-Saxon village, reconstructed on its original site following excavation. (TL 797714.)

Wharram Percy (North Yorkshire): the most famous deserted village site in the United Kingdom, now in the care of English Heritage, who have laid out some of the excavated areas in gravel. Over forty seasons of excavation, however, only about 5 per cent of the village as a whole was dug, so plenty of good earthworks remain, together with the ruins of the church. A good guidebook is available from the post office at Wharram le Street. The site is a walk of about half a mile from the car park at Bella Farm. (SE 858646.)

7
Further reading

General books on deserted villages and landscape history

Aston, M. *Interpreting the Landscape*. Batsford, 1985.

Aston, M., Austin, D., and Dyer, C. (editors). *The Rural Settlements of Medieval England*. Blackwell, 1989.

Atkinson, J.A., Banks, I., and MacGregor (editors). *Townships to Farmsteads: Rural Settlement Studies in Scotland, England and Wales*. BAR 293, 2000.

Baker, A.R.H., and Butlin, R.A. *Studies of Field Systems in the British Isles*. Cambridge University Press, 1973.

Baker, A.R.H., and Harvey, J.B. (editors). *Man Made the Land*. David & Charles, 1973.

Beresford, M.W. *The Lost Villages of England*. Lutterworth, revised edition 1963.

Beresford, M.W. *History on the Ground*. Sutton, revised edition 1998.

Beresford, M.W, and Hurst, J.G. (editors). *Deserted Medieval Villages*. Lutterworth, 1971.

Beresford, M.W., and St Joseph, J.K. *Medieval England – an Aerial Survey*. Cambridge University Press, second edition 1979.

Dyer, C. *Standards of Living in the Middle Ages*. Cambridge University Press, 1989.

Hingley, R. (editor). *Medieval or Later Rural Settlement in Scotland*. Historic Scotland, 1993.

Hooke, D. (editor). *Medieval Villages*. Oxford University Committee for Archaeology, 1985.

Hoskins, W.G. (with Taylor, C.C.). *The Making of the English Landscape*. Hodder & Stoughton, revised edition with additional material 1988.

Muir, R. *Shell Guide to Reading the Landscape*. Michael Joseph, 1981.

Muir, R. *The Lost Villages of Britain*. Michael Joseph, 1982.

Muir, R. *The Shell Guide to Reading the Celtic Landscapes*. Michael Joseph, 1985.

Roberts, B. *The Making of the English Village*. Longman, 1987.

Rowley, T. *Villages in the Landscape*. Orion, 1994.

Sawyer, P.H. (editor). *Medieval Settlement*. Edward Arnold, 1976.

Taylor, C.C. *Village and Farmstead*. George Philip, 1983.

See chapter 8 for journals and periodicals.

Fieldwork

Aston, M., and Rowley, R.T. *Landscape Archaeology*. David & Charles, 1974.

Brown, A.E. *Fieldwork for Archaeologists and Local Historians*. Batsford, 1987.

Hogg, A.H.A. *Surveying for Archaeologists and Other Fieldworkers*. Croom Helm, 1980.

Taylor, C.C. *Fieldwork in Medieval Archaeology*. Batsford, 1974.

Case-studies, excavation reports and detailed work

Austin, D. *The Deserted Medieval Village of Thrislington, County Durham: Excavations 1973–1974*. Society for Medieval Archaeology Monograph 12, 1989.

Bell, R.D., Beresford, M.W., *et al. Wharram Percy: The Church of St Martin.* Society for Medieval Archaeology Monograph 11, 1987.

Beresford, G.T.M. *The Medieval Clay-land Village: Excavations at Goltho (Lincolnshire) and Barton Blount (Derbyshire).* Society for Medieval Archaeology Monograph 6, 1975.

Beresford, M., and Hurst, J. *Wharram Percy: Deserted Medieval Village.* English Heritage, 1990.

Everson, P. *Change and Continuity: Rural Settlement in North-west Lindsey.* RCHME, 1991.

RCAHMS. *Mar Lodge Estate, Grampian: An Archaeological Survey.* RCAHMS, 1995.

Wrathmell, S. *Domestic Settlement 2: Medieval Peasant Farmsteads.* Wharram Percy Monograph 6, York University Archaeological Publications 8, 1989.

The *Annual Reports* of the Medieval Settlement Research Group provide the most comprehensive review of current fieldwork and research into deserted villages (see chapter 8). The Group can also provide up-to-date details of the important series of reports published by the Wharram Research Project on excavations and fieldwork carried out at Wharram Percy, North Yorkshire, over more than forty years. These reports are still appearing.

The Society for Medieval Archaeology (see chapter 8) has published several reports on excavations at deserted village sites in its journal and as monographs.

8
Sources of information

(1) The *National Monuments Records* for England, Scotland, Wales and Ireland can be consulted as follows:

England: c/o English Heritage, National Monuments Record Centre, Kemble Drive, Swindon, Wiltshire SN2 2GZ. Telephone: 01793 414600. Website: www.english-heritage.org.uk

Scotland: c/o Royal Commission on the Ancient and Historic Monuments of Scotland, John Sinclair House, 16 Bernard Terrace, Edinburgh EH8 9NX. Telephone: 0131 662 1456. Website:www.rcahms.gov.uk

Wales: c/o Royal Commission on Ancient and Historical Monuments (Wales), Crown Buildings, Plas Crug, Aberystwyth, Ceredigion SY23 1NJ. Telephone: 01970 621233. Website: www.rcahmw.org.uk

Northern Ireland: c/o Environment and Heritage Agency, Department of the Environment, 5/33 Hill Street, Belfast BT1 2LA. Telephone: 028 9023 5000. Website: www.nics.gov.uk/ehs

Republic of Ireland: c/o Duchas, The Heritage Service, 6 Upper Ely Place, Dublin 2. Telephone: 00353 1647 3000.

(2) *Sites and Monuments Records (SMRs).* Planning authorities have access to an SMR for their area. Check with your local planning department for the one

which covers the area in which you are interested.

(3) *Public Record Office*, Ruskin Avenue, Kew, Richmond, Surrey TW9 4DU. Telephone: 020 8876 3444. This is the central national archive for government and official papers. Website: www.pro.gov.uk

(4) *Council for British Archaeology (CBA)*, Bowes Morrell House, 111 Walmgate, York YO1 9WA. Telephone: 01904 671417. Here is a mine of useful information on where to find local sources, societies and groups. The Council publishes the magazine *British Archaeology*, which includes details of courses, conferences and excavations seeking volunteers. It also maintains a comprehensive index to archaeological information on the Worldwide Web (www.britarch.ac.uk).

(5) *Medieval Settlement Research Group*, c/o S. Coleman, Heritage and Environment Section, Bedfordshire County Council, County Hall, Cauldwell Street, Bedford MK42 9AP. Telephone: 01234 228072. Website: www.britarch.ac.uk/msrg The Group holds regular meetings, conferences and seminars and publishes an annual report that contains details of the latest research on deserted villages.

(6) Finally, three national academic societies with an interest in deserted villages:
Society for Landscape Studies, c/o Dr Della Hooke, 91 Oakfield Road, Selly Park, Birmingham B29 7HL Telephone: 0121 472 4253. Publishes *Landscape History* annually.
Society for Medieval Archaeology, c/o Dr Andrew Reynolds, Institute of Archaeology, 31–4 Gordon Square, London. Publishes *Medieval Archaeology* annually.
Society for Post-Medieval Archaeology, c/o David Gaimster, British Museum, Great Russell Street, London WC1B 3DG. Publishes *Post-Medieval Archaeology* annually.

All three societies also hold seminars and conferences which sometimes include studies of deserted villages. Addresses of academic societies are subject to change. If necessary, contact the Council for British Archaeology (see above) for up-to-date details.

9
Glossary of terms

Assart: clearing or enclosure of waste or common land for agriculture in medieval times (used as a verb or a noun).

Borough, burgh: a settlement which has been granted a licence to hold markets and possesses other privileges.

Clachan: a Gaelic word for a **hamlet** or village in Scotland or Ireland, usually characterised by a lack of recognisable plan.

Common (land): land in which particular people or communities have rights to graze animals, cut turf, collect firewood, etc.

Crofts: enclosed paddocks or orchards attached to village houses.

Fermtoun: a Scots word for a **hamlet**; literally, a 'farm-town', an agricultural settlement.

Furlong: a collection of strips in English open-field agriculture which followed a particular crop rotation; especially characteristic of midland England.

Glebe (land): land belonging to the church, set aside to support a priest.

Hafod: Welsh term for a summer settlement or **shieling**.

Hamlet: a small agricultural settlement without a parish church, but sometimes containing a secondary chapel.

Infield/outfield: a form of open-field agriculture especially characteristic of upland or marginal farming areas. An intensively farmed area around the settlement (infield) was surrounded by an outer ring of land which was periodically left uncropped to recover fertility (outfield).

Kirktoun: a Scots word for a settlement containing the parish church.

Laithe-house, longhouse: combined farmhouse and barn with one end reserved for the family and the other for farm animals.

Messuage: dwelling house with outbuildings.

Milltown, miltoun: a settlement containing a mill.

Open-field agriculture: the most common form of medieval agriculture, in which villagers' lands were held in intermixed strips. Arrangements varied widely across Britain. The expression is often used specifically to refer to the form characteristic of the English midlands in the later middle ages.

Parish: originally, the area whose tithes supported the parish church. In the sixteenth century parish officials were given responsibility for looking after the poor and other matters. (See also **township**.)

Plough team: the oxen which pulled medieval ploughs.

Ridge and furrow ('rig'): the earthwork remains of former fields formed into ridges, which survive in many parts of Britain. Land was ridged for drainage and/or to define strips in open-field agriculture.

Runrig, rundale: types of ridge and furrow characteristic of Scotland and Ireland respectively.

Shieling: a small settlement in mountain or moorland areas occupied only in the summer to make use of hill grazing land.

Toft: an enclosed yard or garden surrounding a village house.

Township: a rural community, *with its farms, fields and other lands and resources.* The boundaries of the township may or may not coincide with those of the **parish** or lordship. The word has no urban connotations, but where a township contained scattered hamlets the 'town' referred to the largest of them.

Vill: a word invented by historians based on the Latin word *villa,* meaning **township**, found in medieval documents.

10
Fieldwork questionnaire

This Fieldwork Questionnaire was produced by the Medieval Settlement Research Group to provide a checklist of things to look out for when exploring deserted village sites. You are welcome to photocopy it or scan it into a computer, but please remember to complete a questionnaire for sites you discover and send the completed version to the local SMR for the area and to the MSRG (see chapter 8). New information is always useful, whether or not the site has been noted previously. If you can send in photographs too, these can be especially valuable.

Completed by .... Date....................

1. Name of county.
2. Name of site (if known).
3. Name of present parish.
4. National grid reference: (a) of site (NB: many of those on the MSRG lists at present relate to a modern farm while they should show the exact location of the deserted village); (b) of medieval church or chapel of village (if any).
5. Name and address of owner(s).
6. Name and address of tenant(s) farming the site.
7. Name and address of nearest inhabited house to the site, if not the same as (6).
8. Remarks and prospects for future preservation of site.

The site
9. At what height above sea level does the site lie, and how does this relate to the surrounding landscape?
10. On what kind of soil does the site lie and what is the geology? (You may find published geology maps helpful for the latter.)
11. If the village is on a slope, in which direction is it facing?
12. Is there a stream or spring nearby?
13. Is the site ill drained? (If not, could this be the result of recent field drainage?)
14. Is there a well on the site, and what material is it lined with?
15. What is the relation of the site to the church (if any)?

The earthworks
16. Are there any earthworks, and if so, over what area do they extend? (Very often they are to be found in several adjacent fields. Mark on the

first plan the fields in which earthworks of the village can be seen.)
17. Is the site sloping, terraced or all on one level?
18. Do the earthworks form a recognisable pattern or are they indistinct and vague?
19. Are the lines of the roads visible? (These usually show as sunken ways.)
20. Can you pick out any distinct house sites? (These are not always seen as buried wall foundations but may be represented by raised platforms; and the positions of hearths may at times be indicated by patches of nettles.)
21. Are the house platforms contained within property enclosures? (These are either banks, buried stone walls or ditches, depending on the geology.)
22. How do these house sites and boundaries relate to the streets?
23. Is the village site defined by a boundary bank and ditch?
24. Are there any castle or moated sites or particularly extensive or prominent house sites in the village, and could they represent the site(s) of the manor house(s)?
25. How does (do) the site(s) of the castle or manor house(s) relate to the village?
26. Is there a village green? (This is usually a relatively level clear area in the village site, sometimes bounded by streets.)
27. Are there any ponds? (There may be a pond on the village green. Ponds will probably have silted up too much today to contain water.)
28. Is there any evidence for post-medieval disturbance of the site, by quarrying or modern ponds, for example?
29. Are there any fishponds, millponds or mill leats nearby?

Ploughed sites
30. If the site is partly or wholly ploughed, how long has this been done and was the site levelled first by a bulldozer?
31. Are earthworks still visible in the ploughed field?
32. Are there any signs of soil marks in the ploughsoil representing ploughed-up buildings, yards and boundaries? Can you make a plan of them?
33. Are there any pieces of worked stone lying in the ploughsoil?
34. Can you collect pottery and other surface finds, bagging them by areas or fields? (If you have a 25-inch map record the field number. If pottery is collected by area, this should give a useful date range for the different parts of the site and make it possible to suggest expansion and contraction within the site, if you can collect enough.)
35. If you visit the site when it is under crop, are there any signs of cropmarks?

Ridge and furrow
36. Is there any ridge and furrow visible near the village? If so, how is it related to the village?

37. Is it straight or curved?
38. What is the width between the tops of the ridges?
39. How high are the tops of the ridges from the bottoms of the furrows?
40. If possible, try to include the outline of any ridge and furrow on your plans.

Plans
1. Extent and outlines of the site in the modern field system.
2. Detailed plans or sketches of earthworks, etc.

Standing buildings
41. List the standing buildings on or near the site and give if possible an approximate estimate of their date.
42. What are the building materials, (a) in the church, (b) in other buildings? Are they local?

The church or chapel
43. Does the church occupy the highest point on the site?
44. Is the church ruined? If so, how much of it still survives?
45. If it is intact, how often is it used?
46. What is the earliest architectural style, e.g. Norman?
47. What is the dominant style? Does this or the size of the church indicate a period of prosperity?
48. Is there evidence of a contraction of the size of the church?
49. To what style does the final period of alteration belong?
50. If the church is a modern building, does it contain any older features such as a font from an earlier church?
51. To what period do the interior ornaments and monuments belong?
52. What are the latest dates for the tombstones in the churchyard?
53. What shape is the churchyard and what is the churchyard boundary made of?

Other buildings of particular interest
54. Are any other buildings of particular interest or early date?

Documentation
55. Do you know of any documents mentioning the site?
56. Name and address of compiler.

Completed questionnaires should be copied to the Secretary of the Medieval Settlement Research Group and to the local Sites and Monuments Record.

Index